Pauline's Puzzlement

A Kid's Book...Not Just for Kids

Steve Kunz

Illustrated by Karen Hargett

ISBN 979-8-88685-740-5 (paperback)
ISBN 979-8-88685-843-3 (hardcover)
ISBN 979-8-88685-741-2 (digital)

Christian Faith Publishing
832 Park Avenue
Meadville, PA 16335
www.christianfaithpublishing.com

Printed in the United States of America

I dedicate this book to my lovely granddaughters, Rebekah Lyn and Chase Marie. You have been the motivating force for me to finish this task. My desire since you were very young has been for you to know Jesus as your Lord and Savior and to live a victorious life in Christ! Keep your eyes on Jesus because He always has His eyes on you!

I love you!

Grandpa Stevie

Acknowledgment

I want to thank my family for their support in this effort. I especially want to thank my wife, Jane Stallard, for helping with proofreading and endless readings of every rewrite. I want to give a huge shout out to my twin sister, Christie Lanning, who gave me many helpful suggestions and rephrasing ideas. I want to thank the Lord for giving me the desire, outline, and the title. I also want to thank my pastor, Jimmy Swaggart, for diligently searching the scriptures and seeking the Lord to understand the sin nature as outlined throughout the Bible, especially in the book of Romans chapters 6, 7, and 8. Pastor Jimmy Swaggart along with Pastor Loren Larson patiently shared on "A Study in the Word" and "The Message of the Cross" on Sonlife Broadcasting Network (SBN) how to have victory over the sin nature in my life. I am eternally grateful for the Apostle Paul and his obedience to the Holy Spirit in giving us this most important doctrine of sanctification. Most importantly, I am thankful to my Lord and Savior, Jesus Christ, for paying the sin debt that I owed but was unable to pay! I love you, Jesus!

Chapter 1

Our story begins, like so many others, with "Once upon a time," but this is where our story takes a remarkable twist!

Due to the fact that all of us could insert our names in the place of Pauline, this story could very well be *our* story. The **"Puzzlement"** I am about to relate happened some time back, but it's still indelibly etched in my mind! This scenario, although played out with different characters at different times and in different places, happens every day somewhere in this magnificent place where we live called LIFE!

We all have or have had a **"Puzzlement."**

Once upon a time, I don't remember the exact date. Hold on a second; now I remember!

My mind is like a steel trap!

OH MY GOODNESS! The thought of that sent a shiver down my spine! It took my mind back to my youth when I narrowly escaped the steel bar of a mousetrap that almost took my life! From that day forward, I learned to appreciate life, and I also became more attentive to my surroundings.

Now getting back to the story I was about to tell.

It was the 18th of December. The year, I honestly do forget, but I do know with absolute certainty that it was a Sunday morning, a week before Christmas.

A young girl named Pauline Princeton found herself in a **"Great Puzzlement!"** Since our story centers around Pauline and her **"Puzzlement,"** I shall call this story…**Pauline's Puzzlement!** Now there's a scoop!

The events I'm about to relate took place in the little village of Summerfield. Summerfield is a former coal mining and farming town smack-dab in the middle of the United States. It's surrounded by fields of corn, soybeans, and wheat. Many years ago, the coal veins ran out. Little by little, after the mine closed, the once bustling town of over two thousand diminished to its current population of five hundred. As the jobs left, so did the people, and with the people, went the businesses. The grocery stores, the bank, the barber and beauty shops, the funeral home, and the blacksmith shop all shuttered their doors. Now only a few businesses remain.

We enter our story through the welcoming, huge, solid wooden doors of the only church that still remains. Crossfire Church was built way back in 1867 by the early settlers. They named it Crossfire Church because they wanted the name to announce to the world that they believed in Jesus and His sacrifice on the cross of Calvary! The name of the church also proclaimed their desire to be empowered, strengthened, and led by the Holy Spirit, just like on the day of Pentecost, when the Holy Spirit lighted on those assembled with tongues of fire above their heads.

Are you ready to learn about the main characters in our story?

Now pay particularly close attention to these characters. You may find yourself identifying with one or maybe parts of all!

You might want to put on a clean pair of socks as you start to walk around in their shoes!

Chapter 2

The title of this story is named after Pauline Princeton, a dark-haired girl who was eleven years old at the time of this story. She always wore her hair in a ponytail; not your normal ponytail, I assure you, but what I call a high ponytail. You know the kind, like the tail on a prancing pony. Pauline's mother fixed it that way every morning, right before breakfast.

Pauline's eyes were a light bluish green, which encouraged those with whom she talked to immediately feel at ease around her.

Rebekah Lyndal was Pauline's best friend. They have been best friends since the first day they met. Rebekah and Pauline are the same age. Rebekah moved to Summerfield from another coal mining town located in the Appalachian Mountains of southeastern Kentucky. The name of that little town is Seco, which is derived from the first letters of the Southeast Coal Company, which owned the town. Interestingly, near the town of Seco is another small town called Kona, which through folklore tells us that a beech tree that stood on the east bank of the Boone Fork had a carving with the inscription DB 1781. The carving is said to have been carved by Daniel Boone, the famous explorer and frontiersman who blazed the Wilderness Road through the Cumberland Gap, which made it possible for the early settlers of our young country to easily cross the Appalachian Mountains. Rebekah has blonde hair and beautiful hazel eyes. Her smile is quick, and her laughter is extremely contagious! As far as we know, a cross word has never passed her lips. Now I'm not saying she's never uttered a cross or angry word; all I can say is that I've never heard one come from her.

The narrator of our story is one of the cutest characters you will ever meet, if I do say so myself! I'm speaking of myself! My name is

Chase Marie Morgan. My friends and family call me Chaser. I will now share one of the greatest experiences of my life.

Oh, my goodness; my heart starts to race just thinking about what I'm about to relate to you!

First, let me give you a description of myself.

To give you as accurate of a description as I can, I will look into this mirror and tell you what I see.

First of all, I'm a girl and quite petite. In fact, I'm extremely small, standing only a little over three inches tall when I stand up on my hind legs. I usually wear a cotton printed dress with lace around the collar and cuffs. Because of my poor vision, I wear wire-rimmed glasses with thick lenses perched on my cute little nose! The color of my beady but cute little eyes is black. I rarely go anywhere without a matching ribbon or a bonnet on my head. My body color is gray, or as the highbrows say, ashen. All in all, I'm very cute! If you haven't guessed, I'm a church mouse!

Yes!

A CHURCH MOUSE!

Normally, church mice are to be quiet, but the "news" I have to tell you is of such magnitude that I'm going to "SHOUT" it from the housetop, or, in my case, the "steeple!"

I want the world to know the good news of Jesus Christ and Him crucified!

Chapter 3

Are you ready? Please be very careful as you walk up these beautiful stone steps that lead to the massive wooden doors of the sanctuary. Once inside, I will show you where this story began. Remember now, this is a house of worship! So please act in a respectful manner!

Okay! Let's go in!

As we walk down the center aisle, look at the beautiful stained-glass windows to your right and left. These windows were handcrafted by Dewey John Rieger, a very talented farmer who lived just a couple of miles south of town. Each window portrays a different scene from the Bible, starting with Genesis chapter 1 and depicting Bible stories through Revelation chapter 22. The center window on the left depicts the birth of Jesus. The three middle windows on the right depict the death, burial, and resurrection of Christ.

Facing the front, you will see the beautiful wooden cross made by master woodworker Franklin Carver of Trenton, with framed pictures on each side of the cross. On the left side of the cross is a picture of Jesus with a lamb gently being carried on His shoulders. The picture on the right shows Jesus seated with children all around Him and one child on His lap! I love these pictures. They've been hanging in the same spot for as long as I can remember.

Let's head downstairs using the door on the right side of the altar.

Now I will give you a play-by-play commentary of what happened on that event-filled day, similar to what you would hear on the radio from a sportscaster describing what was happening at a ball game. The similarity ends there because the story I will tell could affect time and eternity in your life!

It was a gorgeous December Sunday. I was in my usual place. I always stationed myself on top of the upright piano, being careful to stay hidden between the two stacks of hymnals. The wonderful piano came over on a ship with the early settlers who were from Germany. Looking at the piano, you would have to agree that it had seen better days. The varnish had turned dark brown, almost black, and now, because of age, it had a crackly look. Despite having seen better days, the music that flowed from it was amazing! When Miss Viola parked her oversized backside down on that little round piano stool and nimbly positioned her pudgy fingers on those ivory keys, which through time had turned from white to a jaundiced color of yellow, she literally made the piano wake up and sing.

At exactly nine o'clock in the morning, the old bronze church bell began to ring, signaling with its clarion call to one and all, that Sunday school was about to begin! The beautiful bell with its rich tone is said to have been cast at the Stuckstede Bell Foundry, which operated in St. Louis, Missouri, from 1855 until 1931.

8

Another beautiful sound filled the air as youngsters of all ages, as well as many adults, came down the old wooden stairs leading to the classrooms. The echoing sound of shoes clomping on those wooden stairs reverberated throughout the fellowship hall! What a glorious sound it was, music to my little ears!

After everyone had been seated and the Lord's Prayer was recited, it was time to sing our praises to the King of kings and the Lord of lords! Every Sunday morning, the old familiar hymns were sung. This particular morning, we started off with **"The Old Rugged Cross"** and finished with **"Amazing Grace."** I really couldn't see it, but I could certainly feel that something *good* was about to happen.

Believe me. It didn't take long for the shouts of glory to begin!

Chapter 4

Miss Leona was the teacher of the fifth and sixth graders. She had been teaching this age group since she was a teenager. Now, well into her sixties, Miss Leona had made it her lifetime goal to share the gospel with as many children as she could. Over the years, many have expressed that they owe a debt of gratitude to Miss Leona because, without her, they may never have given their hearts to the Lord. As hard as it might be to believe, she was instrumental in bringing over half the town to a saving knowledge of Jesus! Glory to God! That just makes me want to shout!

Miss Leona informed the class that the lesson for today would be about a man named Nicodemus. Nicodemus was a Pharisee and a member of the Sanhedrin, the ruling body of Israel during the time of Jesus. Nicodemus had heard about the teaching of Jesus and quite possibly had even heard Him preach. Nicodemus had a heart that longed to know about God and was pulled like a magnet to Jesus. The things that Jesus spoke about seemed to be deeper and more clearly explained than anything he had ever heard or had been taught! He had a strong desire to meet with Jesus, but because of his position in the synagogue, Nicodemus went to visit Jesus under cover of darkness.

It seems kind of odd that he went to see the Light of the world, Jesus, at night in the cover of darkness, but we are all in a state of darkness before, and as we seek Jesus, even if it is not at night!

Jesus spoke to Nicodemus and explained to him that he *must* be born again!

Jesus answered and said unto Him, verily, verily, I say unto you, except a man be born

**again, he cannot see the Kingdom of God.
(John 3:3 KJV)**

Nicodemus didn't understand that Jesus was not talking about becoming a baby again, but that his spirit and soul needed to be made new because sin had made them unusable to God. The sin nature of Adam and Eve has been passed down through the generations to us. This is called original sin. It has been passed down to us in a similar way that certain physical characteristics are passed down from our parents. Jesus then said to Nicodemus:

For God so loved the world, that He gave His only Begotten Son, that whosoever believes in Him should not perish, but have everlasting life. (John 3:16 KJV)

Sometime after that night, Nicodemus opened his heart to Jesus and was saved! The Lord made a totally new person out of Nicodemus! When he left Jesus, he pondered the words of Jesus and played them over and over in his mind. After he gave his heart to the Lord, he looked the same on the outside, but on the inside, he was a new person. No longer did he look at things as he had before. Now he looked at things from God's perspective. Nicodemus became a follower of Christ! A boldness came upon him, and he was not ashamed to let everyone know he was a follower of Jesus! He was now walking in "the Light," not in "darkness!"

Chapter 5

Something happened to Pauline as she listened to that lesson. I will never forget what happened to Pauline, nor will I forget what happened to me that day!

Miss Leona used the lesson to illustrate to the class the importance of asking Jesus into their heart. She taught that the Bible teaches:

> **For all have sinned, and come short of the Glory of God. (Romans 3:23 KJV)**

With a result:

> **For the wages of sin is death. (Romans 6:23a KJV)**

She then gave them the good news:

> **But the gift of God is eternal life through Jesus Christ our Lord. (Romans 6:23b KJV)**

Jesus took the punishment that we all deserved, and He died for all who will believe in Him! Miss Leona then asked, as she always did, if anyone wanted to ask Jesus into their hearts and be born again. Miss Leona reminded the children that just repeating the words would not save them, but *believing* in their heart what the words were saying would!

No sooner had the question passed Miss Leona's lips, than Pauline's hand shot into the air like a rocket! I wanted to get as close as I could, so I perched myself up on the rim of Pauline's purse to get a closer look. The tears of joy were flowing down Pauline's face. The entire class watched and listened intently as Pauline was instructed to repeat the prayer of salvation that Miss Leona spoke:

Dear God in Heaven,
I come to You
In the name of Jesus.
I'm sorry for my sins,
the way I've lived,
the things I've done.
Please forgive me.
and cleanse me
with Your precious blood
from all unrighteousness.
With my mouth,
I confess
the Lord Jesus.
In my heart,
I believe
that God raised Him
from the dead
and He is alive.
At this very moment,
I accept Jesus Christ
as the Savior of my soul
and I make Him
the Lord of my life.
And according to His Word
which cannot lie,
I'm washed,
I'm cleansed,
I'm forgiven,
I am Saved!

In a moment, in a heartbeat, Pauline's life stepped out of darkness and entered into "the Light!"

She was now *saved* and *born again*.

Pauline became a new creature in Christ! Hallelujah! Glory to God!

As tears flowed down her cheeks, Pauline said, "I love You, Jesus! I love You, Jesus! I love You, Jesus, with all of my heart!"

Now back to me for a second.

In all the excitement, I forgot that I was standing on the rim of Pauline's open purse. I started to jump up and down. Unfortunately, I am not as nimble as I once was. As I came back down from one of my jump-for-joy moves, my foot slipped, and I fell into Pauline's purse. Before I could scamper out, my worst fear happened! In Pauline's excitement and having a strong desire to share the good news with her parents, she snapped her purse shut with me on the inside!

Oh no!

Now *I* was literally in the *dark*!

Chapter 6

One of the greatest adventures of my life was about to begin!

It took a little while for my eyes to adjust to the darkness. I was now experiencing the inside of Pauline's purse. My first thoughts were, *What am I going to do, and what is going to happen to me?* It didn't take long to realize that I was soon to go on the journey of my life! As soon as the thoughts entered my mind, Pauline swooped up her purse and we were on our way! But where were we going? I didn't have a clue!

The purse was swinging back and forth as Pauline hurried into the sanctuary to share the news with her parents. I couldn't see much because the only openings were three small eyelets on each side of the purse that I assume were put there for ventilation in the unlikely event that someone would get trapped inside.

Her parents had just finished shaking hands with Pastor Larson, who was also the adult Sunday school teacher, as Pauline reached their side. With all the swinging of Pauline's purse due to her excitement, I had the most difficult time peeking out the eyelets to see the look on her parents' faces. One thing I can tell you, I could clearly hear the joy and excitement in their voices. I also detected their sighs of relief at the thought of knowing that their child had made the most important decision of her life. When the time comes for her to take her last breath on this earth, she will immediately take her next breath in heaven and be eternally in the presence of God!

Glory to God!

Chapter 7

The ride home to their house, not mine, was a most glorious ride for the Princeton family! I can't say that I had the same feeling; in fact, I was experiencing car sickness for the first time. The ride, in all reality, probably only took a few minutes, but to me, it seemed like it would never end! We finally arrived at 1022 N. Mill St., and I, for one, was more than happy!

Pauline once again swooped up her purse in a very reckless manner; didn't she know what valuable cargo she was carrying? Of course, she had no way of knowing, but I was being knocked around from the proverbial pillar to post! Finally, we, meaning the purse and I, made it along with Pauline to her room. She threw us on her bed (the purse and I) and quickly changed her clothes because she wanted to go to Rebekah's house to tell her about the change that had taken place in her life. I resigned myself to the fact that I was to remain an uninvited guest of the Princetons until next Sunday, when I could hitch a ride back to my home at the corner of Kavanaugh and Wakefield Streets. In the meantime, I knew that I must free myself from this prison.

Remembering the advice Miss Leona gave to the children, **"Call upon Me in the day of trouble; I shall rescue you, and you will honor Me" (Psalm 50:15 KJV).** I started to pray and ask the Lord to give me wisdom and protection in my time of need.

Immediately after Pauline left the room, the Lord gave me wisdom to plan my escape from the clutches of the purse! I very carefully used my sharp teeth to gnaw a few threads that were holding the seam of the purse together. I only had to cut two stitches and gently divide the overlapping pieces of leather apart. I was very careful not to cause more damage to Pauline's purse than necessary. I needed an opening no bigger than the size of a quarter to slip my body through. In less than three seconds, I was FREE. I thanked the Lord!

But now what?

Chapter 8

The Lord impressed upon me to get acquainted with my new surroundings without being detected!

I scurried down from the bed and squeezed under the bedroom door. Pauline's room was on the second floor. It was now time to explore the first floor. Scampering down the lushly carpeted stairs, I reached the foyer. To the right, I could explore the living room with its beautiful fireplace and elegant furniture. To the left was the dining room and kitchen area. Being very hungry, I decided to explore the kitchen to see if I could find a few delicious morsels to eat and something to drink. It had been quite some time since I had anything to eat or drink.

Apparently, someone doesn't like the crust of their toast because next to the sink on a saucer was the most delicious piece. The piece contained a swipe of butter and a dab of orange marmalade! It was delicious, so much better than the stale popcorn the children had strung on the beautiful Christmas tree in the Fellowship Hall of the Church. The faucet had a small *drip, drip, drip* that would easily satisfy my thirst. Now that my hunger and thirst were satisfied, I suddenly realized that I had some other urgent business to take care of. I found a tiny gap at the bottom of the back door. Wasting no time, I ran out to take care of that need, then quickly returned to the safety of the Princeton home.

Chapter 9

As I came around the corner of the dining room that leads to the foyer, Pauline was getting ready to go to her best friend Rebekah's house to share with her the news of her born-again experience! Rebekah had spent the weekend with her grandparents, who live in the neighboring town of O'Fallon, and she had gone to their church this morning. Grandpa Stevie brought her home after they all had lunch at Wally's Diner. Pauline set her purse by the front door while she went into the kitchen to kiss her mother goodbye. I decided to hitch a ride in Pauline's purse—as if I hadn't had enough adventure! I quickly found the unstitched seam and climbed inside. I wanted to see the look on Rebekah's face when Pauline shared her good news!

Pauline threw her purse—and me—into the basket of her bicycle, and away we flew. It didn't take long to get to Rebekah's house since she only lives a few blocks away. I was filled with excitement as I waited for Pauline to share her story with Rebekah. I certainly was not disappointed! Rebekah jumped for joy as she threw her arms around Pauline! Rebekah had been praying for Pauline's salvation since the day she had given her heart to the Lord two months earlier. The girls jumped up and down, all the time clinging to each other! In the confines of my little hideaway, I, too, was jumping up and down with excitement!

The girls were on Christmas break from school. They spent at least a few hours together every day. Life was wonderful for Pauline! In fact, she had never felt so *wonderful* in all her life! Everything she looked at seemed more beautiful and glorious than she had ever realized. The burden of sin, which weighed her down, was now lifted like the proverbial ton of bricks being lifted from her shoulders! Pauline felt more alive than she had ever felt!

Life was truly *wonderful!* The words, "I'm saved! I'm saved!" rolled off her tongue like sweet music sliding off the ivory keys of a grand piano! Nothing compared to the feeling she felt! Pauline was full of glory and had joy unspeakable! Nothing feels better than that!

Pauline was on cloud nine for the next few days. Everything seemed perfect in her world. The Christmas lights seemed to twinkle brighter, and their colors seemed more vibrant. The light snow cover, which was only on the lawn, looked so beautiful and so pure. Little blades of grass were still sticking up, almost in a defiant way, kind of like a young child that doesn't want to go to bed for fear of missing something. The laughter and soft chatter of men, women, boys, and girls passing by on the sidewalk by her house made her smile inside, with a feeling that everything was right in the world. But then! What happened next was totally unexpected and caught Pauline totally off guard.

To celebrate Pauline giving her heart to the Lord, her parents gave her $20 to go to the store and buy whatever she wanted, with a few restrictions that Pauline knew so well. Pauline was beyond thrilled that her parents were so generous with her, especially knowing that her parents had more bills during this time of the year since they always loved to buy perfect gifts for all their relatives and friends. Pauline rode her cute pink bicycle with the white basket that hung down on the front side of the handlebar to Freshour's Drugstore. Pauline loved to ride her bike as fast as she safely could. The wind caressed her face, and her ponytail seemed like it was blown back, almost sticking straight out like the tail end of a weather vane. The brisk air caused her eyes to water, and the tears gently slid down her cheeks.

It didn't take long for Pauline to get to Freshour's Drugstore. You might be wondering where I was during this high-speed bike ride! I was in the safety of Pauline's purse, which she had carefully placed in that cute white basket on the handlebars.

As Pauline entered the store, she was overwhelmed with so many choices. There was an aisle with medical equipment. She looked down the aisle and quickly surmised that she didn't want to spend her money on a walker, cane, or elastic braces for elbows and knees. Looking down the next aisle, she knew immediately that she didn't need any aspirins, medicine for upset stomachs, or ear and eye remedies.

The next aisle showed more promise. It was lined with greeting cards and magazines. As she walked down the aisle, she thought to herself that she really was not in need of cards or magazines.

Finally, she reached the last aisle; it looked like the Promised Land to her. The shelves and display cases were filled with more makeup than she knew existed in the world. Pauline knew that her mom prohibited her from wearing lipstick at her current age, but the colors were so enticing and seemed to be calling out her name. She sensed a small voice in her innermost being saying, *Don't buy the lipstick! Honor your mother's wishes!*

She seemed to hear another voice compelling her to buy the bright pink shade. The voice seemed to be saying to her, *Your mom doesn't realize that you're old enough to wear lipstick; she's just so old-fashioned! All the other girls in the class get to wear lipstick! Their moms are cool and know that we are living in modern times!* Pauline decided to go against that still small voice telling her the right thing to do and decided to listen to the other voice and buy it anyway. She also saw a colorful scarf that would meet her mother's approval.

Looking to the left, her eyes saw the most beautiful hairbrush/comb set with a beautiful hand mirror. When the sweet elderly clerk, Mrs. Freshour, noticed Pauline, she asked her if she needed any help. Pauline shook her head and politely answered no.

Walking up to the beautiful wooden checkout counter, which was lined with several stools that had padded red leather seats and chrome pedestal bases, Pauline placed her desired purchases on the counter. Mrs. Freshour totaled up the items and the total came to $12.94. Pauline gave her the twenty-dollar bill. Mrs. Freshour counted out the change, which should have been $7.06, but Mrs. Freshour gave Pauline, mistakenly, a ten-dollar bill in place of a five-dollar bill. Pauline noticed the mistake but remained silent. She thought, as most people in the world think, that they make lots of money here and it's not my mistake but hers.

The lipstick that she bought, which was not on her mom's approval list, was carefully concealed in an inner pocket of her coat so as to go undetected by her mother.

No sooner had she gone outside, she realized she was wrong for not alerting Mrs. Freshour of the clerical error.

A voice in her head said, Don't worry, the Lord is blessing you today." But once again, that still small voice countered the other voice and said, *No, the Lord is not blessing you. That's stealing!*

Now what am I going to do? she pondered.

What a revolting development this is!

She could have gone back into the store but decided not to. As she rode home, she didn't pedal nearly as fast as when she left for the store. Her mind was seemingly being pulled in two directions.

She now thought of the forbidden lipstick safely tucked on the inside of her coat. *What have I done?* she thought! The Holy Spirit kept dealing with her and convinced her that what she had done was wrong.

Sorrow filled her being.

What am I going to do now? I thought I was saved and would not sin again, but I did! Maybe I should read my Bible more. That's the answer, she thought!

As soon as she got home, she started to read her Bible, keeping her sin hidden from her mother. Reading the Bible didn't seem to remove the feeling of failure that settled in her heart. Pauline tried to push those thoughts into the deep recesses of her mind, but the thoughts of her sin didn't totally disappear.

Chapter 10

A couple of days later, it was gift exchange time between Rebekah and Pauline. I quickly slipped into Pauline's purse, so as not to miss a second of the fun between Pauline and Rebekah. Once again, we were on our way on Pauline's pink bicycle. Well, it didn't take long for the joy to turn to sorrow. What should have been an exciting and wonderful experience soon became anything but! It started off great! Rebekah opened her gift from Pauline first. It was a beautiful silver charm bracelet with a volleyball charm to signify Rebekah's favorite sport. Rebekah was overjoyed with the *perfect* gift, and the huge smile on her face expressed her satisfaction. Pauline then opened her present from Rebekah. It was a scarf, mittens, and stocking cap set! Everything was pink, except for a little white fringe on the cuffs of the mittens. Personally, I thought they were to die for!

What happened next, no one in the room expected, especially Rebekah!

Pauline tossed the presents aside. The expression on her face revealed her dissatisfaction with the gifts. Rebekah was quick to notice the look on Pauline's face and said, "Don't you like the gifts I bought you? I was so sure that you would!"

Pauline tried to reassure Rebekah that the gifts were fine, but her answer, "They're fine!" didn't quell the knowing that Rebekah felt in her heart. An uneasy feeling seemed to fill the room. Embarrassed and realizing she wasn't good at disguising her disappointment in the gifts, Pauline said that she needed to get home. Both girls knew that wasn't the real reason, but they politely said goodbye as Pauline, her gifts, and I headed out the door. "Now I've really made a mess of things! I just insulted and hurt the feelings of my best friend!" Pauline said with a tearful voice.

Being filled with guilt and pain, Pauline threw her gifts and her purse—filled with precious cargo, me—in the basket, hopped on her bike, and pedaled tearfully home.

As she rode, she kept repeating, "How could I have been so mean and thoughtless? How could I have been so mean and thoughtless? How could I have been so mean and thoughtless?"

I just got saved on Sunday morning! I thought that once a person got saved, they could never sin again! What happened? Maybe I didn't really get saved? I have a **"Puzzlement"** *that I just don't have the answer to.* As she pondered those thoughts, she broke into uncontrollable sobbing.

Chapter 11

Pauline carelessly dropped her bike in the flower bed! After fumbling to get the key properly inserted into the lock, she forcibly opened the front door, throwing her purse—and me—on the floor next to the umbrella stand. Pauline went on a desperate search for her mother. My head was still spinning from the hard landing and the sight I had just witnessed at Rebekah's house, when I heard a loud, panicky voice piercing the air! Pauline started crying out for her mother!

"Mom! Mom! I didn't think that people who were born again ever sinned! I was saved just the other day, and now I feel like I am sinning at every turn! What am I going to do now?" The words flowing out of her mouth were faster than a machine gun!

She started to cry, and the tears flowed like a river. Her whole body uncontrollably shook with the feeling that was inside.

"Mom… Mom!" Pauline yelled for her mother.

I waited with baited breath for Pauline's mother to come to Pauline's rescue. Her mother came running into the room expecting to see someone hurt or something broken. Little did she know that someone was hurt and something was broken, but not the way she expected. Rebekah had her feelings hurt and her heart was also broken. Pauline was ashamed and confused. Her thoughts were spinning so fast in her head that she couldn't understand how she could have let the Lord down through her unpremeditated actions!

Pauline's mother quickly wrapped her arms around Pauline to calm her down enough to be able to explain what was going on.

"Slow down, Pauline! Slow down, Pauline! What's the matter? What happened?"

"Oh, Mom, something just happened that upset me and REALLY upset Rebekah. I have **A Puzzlement!"**

"A what?" Her mother asked.

*A **what?*** I thought!

"A Puzzlement!" said Pauline.

"Mom, I just don't understand what is happening. I know I was saved a few days ago, but because of what I did today, I'm not sure."

"What happened?" Mom asked.

"The day started with my heart filled with joy and excitement because of the new feeling that was inside me. But in just a few minutes, the joy of living for the Lord changed and got worse and worse. As you know, I went to Rebekah's to exchange Christmas presents. She loved my gift to her! I knew she would! But when I opened her gift to me, a different me seemed to take over! I tried to control my reaction, but I wasn't good at disguising my disappointment with the gifts Rebekah gave me! The expression on my face telegraphed to Rebekah that I didn't really like the gift she gave me. I didn't actually say how disappointed I was, but the look on my face left no doubt! When Rebekah asked me if I liked the gift, I gave a half-hearted response. Rebekah knew instantly that I didn't like the gifts, and she started crying. I have never felt so sad as when I saw the sadness on her face. She is my best friend, and I didn't mean to hurt her feelings."

Pauline continued, "When she started crying, all I could do was to look down at the scarf, hat, and mittens in my hands and wonder how I could have been so thoughtless and hurtful to the best friend I have! In fact, the more I looked at the gifts, I kind of liked them more and realized how much thought Rebekah put into finding the gift that she thought I would love. Mom, Rebekah is my best friend! I didn't mean to hurt her feelings! When Rebekah started crying, I immediately knew that I had done something really bad. Mom, I thought that after we got saved, we wouldn't do things that hurt Jesus and others. Why did I act so mean today? Am I really saved…or not? This is my **'Puzzlement.'** Why did I do something I didn't want to do? Why didn't I do the right thing?"

Mother said, "I like the word **'Puzzlement,'** Pauline. The **'Puzzlement'** you experienced today is not something new or something unique. It is something that has happened and continues to happen to all born-again Christians. The problem is easy to see, but the remedy is not understood by most. I'll try to explain it to you, and I hope that the Holy Spirit will open your heart to understanding. But before I begin to explain this to you, why don't we pray?"

Pauline's small hands reached out as her mother tenderly enfolded them into hers. With their heads bowed, Pauline's mother began to pray: "Dear Lord, please help Pauline understand and also help me to explain this great truth of the 'cross,' which is the foundation of all truth. Thank you once again for providing us with your wonderful plan of salvation. In Jesus precious name we pray. Amen."

Chapter 12

Pauline's mother continued to hold her daughter close as she started to speak. "Before I begin to explain *the message of the cross*, let's do a little review of your understanding of a few basic truths. Number one, what does it mean to be born again, Pauline?"

"Mom, I think that to be born again means to have your sins taken away by Jesus. To have your name written in the *Lamb's Book of Life*. It also means that when I die, I will be with Jesus forever. To be born again means we are saved by grace, not by works. I also think it means that we will never sin again, but I did! Was my thinking wrong?"

"Darling, you are correct on most of what you believe, but the last statement needs a little correction. Before we are saved, we have two natures or personalities: the human nature and the sin nature. The human nature is simply our personality and how we react to outward circumstances, whether good or bad. The sin nature is our nature that wasn't originally planned for mankind but entered Adam and Eve when they disobeyed the instructions of God. The sin nature has been passed down through the generations, and it has a destructive quality that causes us to do things that go against God. The Bible calls it sin. Our willpower, or our desire to keep from sinning, is not strong enough to resist sin through our own efforts and ability. When we ask Jesus to forgive us of our sins and be the Lord of our life, we are *born again* or *saved*. When we are saved, we then receive the divine nature, making a total of three natures: human, sin, and the divine."

She continued, "The divine nature is the Holy Spirit taking up residence in us, desiring, encouraging, and striving to lead us in the ways of God! Most people believe that the sin nature leaves when we are born again. In reality, the sin nature does not leave but becomes dormant, kind of like a sleeping bear. A sleeping bear, or in other words, a hibernating bear, causes no problems for those that encounter him. God's desire is for the sin nature to remain dormant, just like the bear, causing us no problem! The Bible says we are to be dead to sin, but it does not say that sin is dead. Once again, think of the hibernating bear. He is just sleeping and not dead. If we don't keep our focus, or in other words, our eyes on Jesus and what He did for us at the cross, we allow this sin nature to wake up and rear its mean old ugly head, just like the bear, only worse!

Chapter 13

"You mentioned the word *grace* in your answer. That brings me to my next question. Pauline, what does *grace* mean?"

Pauline thought for a moment, and then cautiously said, "I think that grace is a gift from God that I didn't earn or deserve. Is that right?"

"That's correct, Pauline! Grace is a gift from God that none of us can earn. It is extended to us every time we ask for help or forgiveness from God, and many times, grace is given even when we don't ask! When we sin, the Holy Spirit—remember, He has now taken up residence inside us—speaks to our hearts that we have gone against the will of God. We call that being under conviction. When we feel that way, we are to immediately ask the Lord to forgive us, and He will extend His grace to us."

Pauline's mother added, "Many times, we ignore the Holy Spirit because we are not used to listening to and trusting in Him to guide our every action. Up to the time of our salvation, we had lived our lives trusting in ourselves or others to help us make the right decisions. After salvation, we must rely on the Holy Spirit, Who is God, to help us make decisions. God has *nothing* for sale! We can't work hard enough or do enough good deeds to merit the grace of God! God gives us grace because of His *goodness*, not ours! Now we will address your **'Puzzlement!'** Did you know that the Bible addresses the same **'Puzzlement'** that you have?"

"It does?" Pauline said in amazement.

"The solution to your **'Puzzlement'** is found in the Bible, and we label it 'The Message of the Cross!' In fact, 'The Message of the

Cross' is woven throughout the entirety of the Bible, from Genesis through Revelation. I'm going to relate to you, Pauline, a story from the Bible about a man who not only had 'a **Puzzlement**' similar to yours but also a similar name. His name was the Apostle Paul."

Chapter 14

"Sometime shortly after Paul was saved, he experienced the resurgence, or the reawakening, of the sin nature in his life. In other words, he got saved, and shortly thereafter, he started to sin again. He was totally devastated by this experience. This **'Puzzlement'** is recorded in the book of Romans, chapter 7. Paul doesn't tell us what sin or sins he committed, but we do know that he didn't like it and that it was a great problem that he wanted out of his life. He also felt so bad that he worried about the condition of his soul if this problem continued. What Paul didn't realize, but would be taught by the Holy Spirit, was that he had shifted his faith from what Jesus did for him at the cross. When his faith was shifted to anything but the cross of Christ, the Holy Spirit was, in a sense, handcuffed to help him overcome the sin in his life.

"Think of this, Pauline! We have absolutely no power to defeat sin. If we could save ourselves, Jesus would have stayed in heaven and just told us not to sin. We know that this was not the way the sin problem was addressed. We know that it took a perfect sacrifice, Jesus, to pay the sin debt that we all owed! His sacrifice on the cross of Calvary made it possible for all who repent of their sin and accept that sacrifice will be saved. Sometime after Paul got saved, he had a problem with sin. Through the teachings in the Bible, we understand that his faith had shifted to something other than the finished work of Christ on the Cross, but to where did he shift his faith?

"Remember that earlier I said that Jesus was the only one that could take away sin? Now Paul had to learn that valuable lesson! He had shifted his faith from Jesus to himself, thinking that now that he was saved, he could defeat sin through his own efforts and ability. He thought he was now strong enough to resist sin. He either didn't know or forgot that all his strength came from Jesus and what he did at the cross. Sometime later, the Holy Spirit would give Paul the words, 'When I'm weak, He is strong.' The Bible relates it this way:

> **Therefore, I take pleasure in infirmities, in reproaches, in necessities, in persecutions, in distresses for Christ's sake: for when I am weak, then am I strong. (2 Corinthians 12:10 KJV)**

"Paul thought, just like you:

> **For that which I do I allow not: for what I would, that do I not; but what I hate, that do I. (Romans 7:15 KJV)**

"In other words, Paul was asking the same question you are now asking: 'I don't understand why I do the things I don't want to do, and don't do the things that I want to do! Why can't I always do the right thing?' It bothered him so much that he cried out, **"O wretched man that I am! Who shall deliver me from the body of this death?" (Romans 7:24 KJV).** He felt that if he continued sinning, that it would kill him!

"During the time of the apostle Paul's writing of the words from **Romans 7:24**, he was in the city of Corinth. Being led by the Holy Spirit, he felt compelled to write a letter to the believers in Rome. Paul wanted to share what he had experienced and what remedy the Holy Spirit had given him. No doubt, he had heard of or witnessed a type of torture that was used by the Romans of that day. The torture consisted of a convicted criminal having the dead body of another individual, probably another criminal that had just died, strapped to his body until the disease of the dead body was passed to the living criminal, resulting in his death. This was generally a slow, stinking, painful, and horrifying type of punishment. The weight of sin on a saved person can make a person cry out, wanting the disgust and shame of sin to be removed!

"Paul was realizing that his own strength was powerless to defeat the sin nature. He sought God for the answer, which is where we should also go with all our questions and problems. Pauline, keep in mind that the letters and books of the Bible were not originally written with chapters and verses numbered like we have in the Bible today. The translators of the Bible used a numbering system which helps us locate a particular chapter or verse.

"When Paul wrote this letter to the Romans, keep in mind that he wrote just like we would write a letter today. Although I think there needs to be a little clarification, Pauline. His letters in the Bible were written just a little differently than how we write letters, due to the fact that these letters were inspired or told to him by the Holy Spirit. You might say that God instructed every word that he wrote. They were, and are, the words of God. God went through the vocabulary in Paul's mind and chose the precise word that Paul was to write down. That is why we call the Bible the inspired Word of God!

"Now, I'm going to try to simplify this for you, Pauline. Paul realized that he was powerless through his own willpower to stop sinning. He realized that there was a law that was greater than his willpower that did not allow him to overcome his problems! That law is described in **Romans 8:2.** It is the law of **sin and death.** Man has no power in himself to overcome the law of **sin and death.** But the Holy Spirit showed Paul that there is a law that is greater than the law of **sin and death.** It is the law of the **spirit of life.** It's described this way in **Romans 8:1–2 (KJV):**

> **There is therefore now no condemnation to them which are in Christ Jesus, who walk not after the flesh, but after the Spirit. For the Law of the Spirit of Life in Christ Jesus, has made me free from the law of sin and death.**

"Paul learned that his willpower was not the answer to his sin problem, even though he was born again and his sin debt had been paid by Christ. He knew that his original sin condition was taken care of at the cross! Now he learned that when sin reared its ugly head, he still needed it to be taken care of by looking to the cross of Calvary! The lesson he learned was that the cure for all sin is obtained 'by placing our trust exclusively in what Jesus did on the cross. We have always been, and always will be, powerless to take sin out of our lives! That responsibility belongs to Jesus, and Jesus alone! He doesn't need or require our help! The only thing required of us is that we keep our focus on the finished work of Christ at the cross!

"Paul was instructed by the Holy Spirit to keep his focus or his attention on the finished work of Christ at all times. The Lord told him to keep his eyes on the 'cross,' not the wooden beam but what it represented. When we remind fellow Christians to keep their focus on the cross, we are reminding them to remember what Christ did on the cross on their behalf. It is like when someone says, 'Remember Pearl Harbor.' They are not saying we are to think of the idyllic bay in Hawaii, but of the horrific attack on the United States Naval fleet by the Japanese that caused us to enter World War II. Similarly, when we say, 'Remember the Alamo,' we want the listener to remember the battle fought there, not the tourist attraction or the buildings there.

"The cross was where Jesus died for our sins. Paul was to focus on what Christ did for him at Calvary: Jesus paying the price for Paul's sins and ours. The Lord showed Paul that He did it all for us. All we have to do is receive the gift of God. That is why it is called a gift. Think about it, Pauline. Do you have to do anything to earn a gift?"

"No, Mom, I just have to receive it."

"Well, Paul learned that when he kept his eyes on Jesus, the sin nature, that big ugly bear we talked about earlier, would just keep right on snoozing and cause him no problem. But when Paul took his eyes off of Christ and tried to keep the laws himself or try to help Jesus in a certain situation, that bear, the sin nature, would wake up 'bad' and 'mad!' Then all sorts of problems would be created!"

Chapter 15

"The apostle Paul used the term *in Christ, in Him,* or some form of this, about 170 times in his letters. If the Lord tells us something once, it is of great significance. So it stands to reason that if he tells us 170 times, it must be of the utmost importance! When Paul tells us to stay in Christ, he is telling us to stay focused on Jesus and what he did for us at the cross. In other words, we are to keep our faith anchored in what Jesus did for us at Calvary. Pauline, do you understand why you acted so badly today at Rebekah's?"

"Yes, I now realize that my eyes were not on Christ. I also know that when I keep my eyes on Jesus and what He did for me at the cross, the Holy Spirit will give me help in resisting sin, resulting in sin being no problem in my life. But when my eyes are not on Jesus, sin will be a BIG PROBLEM!"

"Pauline, I think your '**Puzzlement**' is now solved."

"Right, Mama! 'Puzzlement' solved. I can't wait to tell Rebekah that I'm sorry for the way I treated her today and tell her what I learned. Can I go over to Rebekah's right now?"

"Yes, sweetheart, I think that would be a great idea."

"Mom, there's just one more thing I need to tell you. Do you remember the $20 you gave me after I got saved?"

"Yes, Pauline, I remember. What do you want to tell me about that?"

"Well, I need to talk to Mrs. Freshour. She gave me $5 too much in change when she checked me out! Would it be alright to go to the drugstore tomorrow? I need to make things right with Mrs. Freshour."

"Certainly, dear, that's exactly the right thing to do. You learned some very valuable lessons today!"

"Oh, Mom, one more thing. Do you think you could keep this beautiful tube of bright pink lipstick that I bought until I'm old enough to wear it? Sorry, I disobeyed you and didn't listen to the Holy Spirit telling me not to buy it!"

"I'll be happy to keep the lipstick for you, and I forgive you, Pauline," Mother said.

"Oh, and Mom! Thanks, I love you! I'll be home at suppertime."
"You're welcome, Pauline, and I love you too."

Chapter 16

I couldn't wait to hear what Pauline would tell Rebekah, so I scurried into Pauline's purse and hitched a ride to Rebekah's. At first, Rebekah didn't want to hear anything that Pauline had to say, but Miss Leona's voice rang in her head, reminding her to forgive those that hurt you.

Soon, her heart melted, and she forgave Pauline.

The girls hugged and went to Rebekah's room to look at her Christmas presents.

The girls were still friends!

I stayed in the purse for the entire week, only leaving to find something to eat or take care of my other needs.

I was happy to have witnessed such a miracle of grace.

But now I was ready to head back to the quiet little church on the corner of Kavanaugh and Wakefield Street. Well, *mostly* quiet, except on Sunday mornings, when the sound of small voices and Sunday shoes racing down the old wooden stairs fills the air.

"Puzzlement" SOLVED!

Praise the Lord!

A LIFE OF VICTORY IN THE FINISHED WORK OF CHRIST!

NOT THE END, BUT THE BEGINNING!

Keep your eyes on Jesus because He always has His eyes on you!

About the Illustrator

Karen Hargett is a self-taught artist, born and raised in Texas. She has always had a natural desire to create and has been involved in arts and crafts most of her life. It was in her 40's when she began riding horses that the heart of her talent revealed itself. Her love for her horse, the demands of an excellent horse trainer, and the deep satisfaction of "getting it right" at the end of a hard day of training became a driving force in her art. She became passionate with her graphite drawings and pastel paintings in "getting it right." With people and animals, she feels that it is most important to capture what the eyes reveal – "that is what makes a painting come alive."

While Karen is passionate about painting animals, she feels a special connection with each and every painting. Whether it is a pet, a person, wildlife, landscapes, or a still life she enjoys using her God given talent in bringing it to life.

Karen's paintings and drawings can be found in collectors' homes, not only across the United States, but from Australia to Scotland as well. Several of her pieces have been featured in Mike Sibley's Starving Artist's "The Editor's Choice." Also, Karen's pastel "All My Marbles" was featured in the Reader's Digest "Drawing & Sketching Secrets" book in working with still-life subjects.

Karen's work may be found on her website to www.KarenHargettFineart.com

Artist Statement

What a joy it is to be able to look at what God has created and then try to describe it on a piece of paper or canvas with pencils, pastels or paint!

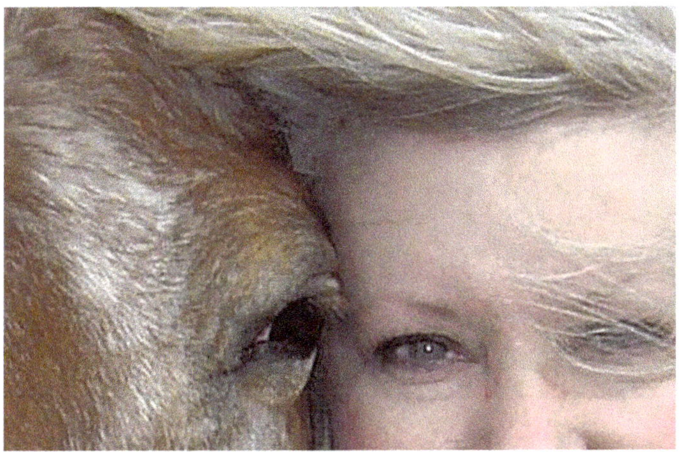

About the Author

Steve Kunz, aka Grandpa Stevie, was born and raised in southern Illinois, just east of the Mississippi River. Steve is a proud husband, father, and grandfather. Steve is a first time author, former educator, foundry man, also has experience in the fast food distribution business. He is an ordained minister, Children's Church Minister and Bible Study Teacher, former Police Chaplain. Steve grew up in a traditional liberal church, not hearing the plan of salvation, as outlined in the Bible until he was in early adulthood. Steve accepted Jesus as his Lord and Savior when he was 33 years old. Steve is fond of saying that he was radically lost and is now radically saved with a burden to share the Gospel of Jesus Christ with as many as possible. Shortly after Steve's born-again experience, he was disappointed with himself because sin reared its ugly head in his life. He diligently sought for answers to why he continued to struggle with sin. Around the year 2000 he became acquainted with the "Message of the Cross", which showed him how to have Victory over the sin nature as outlined in the Book of Romans. Thoughts of writing this book had been on his heart since 2004, when he felt that the Lord was compelling him to write "Pauline's Puzzlement". He also believes that the Lord gave him the title of the book.